MW01204514

TONIGHT I DIE

I DIE

A Journey From Death To Life

J.W. LINDER

Table of Contents

Disclaimer: I do not advise doing any of the outlandish things mentioned in this story in your pursuit of peace for your soul and/or deliverance from an addiction. This just happens to be what God used to rock my world and open my eyes. I welcome you to walk with me through the story of my escape from hell as my eyes are opened to the naked reality of life.

"Jesus did not let him, but said, "Go home to your own people and tell them how much the Lord has done for you, and how he has had mercy on you."
Mark 5:19

Introduction

Where am I now? Where was I then? Where did my story originate? A lot of those questions will not be answered in detail here. What you will find is an amazing story of a crazy adventure mixed with pride and a lonely loner being aggressively pursued by a loving Father. This part of my story occurred over twenty-two years ago. I have come a long way since then. If someone were to look at my life today, they would have no way of knowing about my rebellious past. I have shared this story openly over kitchen tables and once or twice in a small church service but have never aggressively pursued telling my testimony until now.

My main goal in making this book available is to glorify God and praise Him for His goodness, faithfulness, patience with sinful man, and His great love for us despite our many flaws. I have been reluctant in the past to share a very checkered past. I step forward in boldness today to share my testimony with the hopes that you will soon be sharing yours also.

My second goal is to shout from the rooftops that God is real, God is good, and God wants you to know Him. I am a professional. I am a highly successful individual.

I have a very checkered past, but I am winning in life. You can win too. I am devoting my life to helping others win beyond their wildest dreams.

A God I did not believe in came to me in an undeniable way, gave me a simple, clear instruction, and I refused to listen. I finally listened after six more months of self-induced hell. Regardless of how long you have been suffering, you can begin the healing process now by finding a quiet place and stopping long enough to listen. Learning from mistakes is a key part of a successful life. I do not know about you, but I like to learn from others' mistakes rather than my own. A lot of my pain was avoidable. I share my journey with the hopes that something can be gleaned from the story that will help you in your journey.

Angels Cry

I'm on the ground again
Far beyond the skies
I sin and
Angels cry

I used to be a young man
Life's riches were my own
Found freedom behind sharp bars
Now I'm reaping all I've sown

I'm on the ground again
Far beyond the skies
I sin and
Angels cry

It seems I've come to treasure
These pain-filled screams within
My heart's beggin' me to fight
But my body wants the monkey to win

I'm on the ground again
Far beyond the skies
I sin and
Angels cry

This trashing sea is filled with hate
Here in all my dreams have died
Still God's tears whisper hope
His love keeps me alive

Insight:

I have messed up again. My body is lying in the dust of life, but my mind is free and flying wildly into the unknown. Sharp bars are the needles and drugs that controlled my every waking moment. We often learn to love our pain. The pain makes a fleeting pleasure that is much more enjoyable and much more desirable. My lifestyle has killed every good thing in my life. I have no other desire other than more self-destruction. Somehow, I know that God is there and that He is asking me to call on Him.

CHAPTER 1

Locked In A Cage Of Needles And Grass

Dawn was still far away on an early morning on November 1, 1998. The smell of freshly cooked meth lingered in the air around the humble abode on main street USA.

Metallica's "For Whom The Bell Tolls" roared through the otherwise silent neighborhood to offer an unholy welcome for a most awesome, most holy, and most unlikely visitor.

I was minding my own business, unapologetically disturbing the peace, smoking a joint, and rolling the last needle of meth between my skeleton-like fingers when the awesome presence of God Almighty rolled into my house.

It would be easy to try and discredit my experience and chalk it up to an active imagination. It would be easy to say, "This guy was stoned, probably been up for days, and he was just tweaked out and seeing things that were not there." I'll give you that, and I have argued with myself in the same manner. However, I can promise you that I had hundreds of deep hallucinatory experiences prior to this that have been thoroughly implanted in my mind, and this was nothing compared to anything I had ever known. This was not from the drugs. This was the beginning of a supernatural and radical deliverance from addiction.

Up to this point of no return, I was a skeptic, and I do not tell my story lightly. It is off the wall; I know that fully. If I did not personally know the absolute validity of my story, and its potential for life change for those in similar circumstances, then I would by no means be putting my closeted skeletons out for the world to see. If you can make your way through my very tall tale, I think it will be easy to justify that I truly had this experience and, even more so, possibly prepare the road for an experience of your own if you have not met the Living God yet.

Wasted Eagles

Wasted eagle
Creations of our own we were
Masters of our own demise
Saying evil feels good
Decay, destroy me
I ain't afraid to die

Alone, alive, all lies
Daring to be damned
Never known
Wasted eagle,
I remember you
Wasted eagle
These tears I cry for you

Always taking what we wanted
Always needing something more
Blinded by the darkness
No cause and no remorse

Alone, alive, all lies
Daring to be damned
Never known
Wasted eagle,
I remember you
Wasted eagle
These tears I cry for you

I look back on the good times
But I don't miss the pain

Heart held with dead hands
I often wonder if you ever found
Freedom from those chains

Insight:

We refused to listen to anyone about anything. We were wise in our own eyes and determined that everything in our lives would be the opposite of what anyone else considered the "right" way. We were immortal in our own eyes. We never took time to know our Creator; we even mocked Him. I look back on my friends and think of them with tears, the Wasted Eagles. I escaped. I remember the lessons of the past and refuse to entertain returning to that lifestyle. I wonder if my friends ever found true life.

CHAPTER 2
How Did I Get Here?

Maybe some of you can relate to my situation. I started drinking heavily, huffing various chemicals, and smoking weed regularly at around twelve. But I always maintained that I would never use any hard drugs, and I sure would never be a junkie. At the age of seventeen, one of my girlfriends introduced me to her meth-dealing daddy, who introduced me to the needle, and I was hooked.

Over the years, I had tried many times to quit meth. It seemed that every time I would try to quit, access to drugs would become more convenient than ever. I always considered myself a good guy that always tried to help others and tried not to hurt others. But looking back, I can see that I was selfish to the core and full of misplaced pride.

I never really believed in God. I could not see, hear, feel, or touch God. Why should I believe? I often wondered about the existence of a higher power. I prayed a simple forgive me prayer now and then. Just enough talk to help cover any possible consequences of my hellion lifestyle. I was even bold and prayed on occasion,

"Thanks, God, for the party! Forgive me if you can." I figured there was about a one percent chance that there was something else out there. I had written many songs about the follies of Christianity. I would look at all the denominations and all the other religions along with all the infighting and hypocrisy and easily blow religion off. I had a few songs that mocked Christians and boldly proclaimed that "I would be a saint" if God would just show me what that really meant and how to do it.

Silence Me

You're wondering where are my tears
As you stand and scream I'm alone
My face may seem far from there
But your eyes are on a god of stone

I speak, but you silence me
When will you turn and ask for my mercy
I reach, but you run away
Why don't you stop and seek my embrace

You swear the fault lies in me
But my love does not fade away
Just open your eyes, and you'll see
I cry out to you night and day

At night I ponder your escape
I weep and long to call you friend
Just turn from these wicked ways
I'll gladly restore your innocence again

Now you want to see the timeless
Since time has taken its toll
Search no more—I'm right here
Run no more—find freedom from your fears

Insight:

God is speaking here. We wonder why He is not crying openly over us and our devastated lives. We refuse to acknowledge His existence because He is not revealing himself to us in a common human way (i.e., face to face as a man). Because of this, we look at idols that we can touch and feel with our five senses. We worship people and our own desires. God speaks constantly, but we refuse to listen because He is not speaking in a way that makes sense to our "logical" mind. He longs to help us, to be with us, to reveal himself to us. He is eagerly waiting to forgive us.

CHAPTER 3

I'll Never Be A Junkie

We have all heard to never say "never." At the time of God revealing Himself to me, I had been addicted to injecting meth for several years. I had tried to quit many times to no avail. Life was good when I was high. Life was a party. I had owned the meth monkey for over six years. He took up residence with me in 1992 when I met a girl who had a meth pusher for a daddy. I would do a line or two but never really liked it much. One day he said, "Let me hit you with the needle. You'll like it…" He did, and I did like it. That day the monkey became my best friend, my worst enemy, and would soon be my greatest desire even above life itself. But in late 1998, I was nearing the end of my rope. Many of my friends were dead or in prison. I had been prepared to die for many years. From my early teenage years, I lived life with the certainty that I had to party hard because I was going to die at around 23 years of age. Little did I know that God Almighty was going to begin the process of my living death on my 23rd birthday! Maybe the devil knew just how much time he had to kill me off before I learned the truth?!

Through the meth years, death seemed to become more and more inviting with every night spent peering out the windows. There were times where I would sit with a hatchet in one hand and a bat in the other, waiting for the law to bust down my door. It's amazing what over a hundred hours with no sleep, no food, and minimal fluid intake will do to the mind.

As I neared my 23rd birthday, my world began to crumble. I had always been very dependent on relationships with others and struggled with loneliness and emptiness from a very young age. My most recent girlfriend had left me with a new baby inside her belly, and with each passing day, I just seemed to feel the pressure of being more and more alone. I felt very alone and empty even though I was surrounded by close friends on a daily basis.

Things were changing in me because what had once worked to numb me was no longer working. No matter how hard I tried to smoke or inject away the pain, I could not. The fix that had always preserved my sanity seemed to have reached the end of its rope, and the physical and mental bill collectors were at my door demanding my peace and sanity. The hand of death grew heavier in my mind. In the last months of my addiction, I became afraid to even have a bed in my house because I was certain I would die. I soon developed a fear of dying in my sleep and removed all of the beds from my home to make sleep very inconvenient. Looking back, I see that God was slowly softening up my rock-hard heart for the big day when he would stop by.

Everyone knew my house. The doors were never locked, the fridge was always full, the weed was in the top drawer—just do not smoke the last joint. Being alone was not the issue, but an all-consuming and ever-growing emptiness and loneliness was. I know that does not make any sense. But my issue was an issue we were all born with, and it was burned deep in my soul. Looking back, I see how the trail of poison and empty pleasures were used to lead me away from the real source of, and the only pure, fuel for my desires. It has been said that our desire for more is God-given. He is endless and will have endlessly more to offer for eternity. When those desires are pushed off on the things of this world, we will always be disappointed. As some of you surely know by now, the pleasures of this world are never "enough."

"As water reflects the face, so one's life reflects the heart. Death and Destruction are never satisfied, and neither are human eyes." Proverbs 27:19-20

Welcome To My Want

My toil has brought me great gain
But I'm drowning in endless pain
More, give me more—screams the beast within
Horde, horde, you can't afford to give

In the absence of my faith,
I've left true wealth behind
Lust has broken me to pieces,
empty hands are all that's mine

Welcome to my want
I'm never satisfied
I hunger night and day
Though I pile my pleasures high
So take all that you want
But if you're smart, just walk away
Yea, you're welcome to my want
But be warned the price is great

The void inside grows deeper everyday
Living out these lies proves I'm insane
I would run away, but I'm afraid to die
I dangle from the hope that someday I'll find life

When we mingle with the slain
Their wicked ways entice
Feed this forbidden hunger
Stealing fire to hide the night

Welcome to my want
I'm never satisfied
I hunger night and day
Though I pile my pleasures high
So take all that you want
But if you're smart, just walk away

Insight:

My wealth has brought a great deal of comfort and pleasure but also has somehow brought an unrelenting pain inside. I have it all but somehow need more. I cannot give anything to others; I need more for myself. My lifestyle of refusing to give has robbed me of the true treasures in life. I have it all, but I have absolutely nothing because the heart of my being is empty and void and crying for more continuously. I have created my own hell, and it looks very enticing. I am luring you toward me so that I can take everything from you, but I am also trying to start the process of redemption by telling you to stay far away from my folly in life.

CHAPTER 4
An Uninvited Guest

Let's go back to the wee morning hours of November 1, 1998. I was sitting in my house minding my own business when the undeniable presence of Almighty God flooded my home. I had a "Christian" buddy, who was also a junkie, with me that night as a witness to the event. When the heavy presence, which I had never heard of or experienced but was clearly God, flooded my home from above, I was completely consumed with fear. Suddenly I was perfectly aware, with no room for doubt, that there was a living God and that he was literally standing in my dungeon of debauchery and all things evil. He was there to see me....

At once, I thought I knew why he was there. To take me to HELL! If anyone deserves hell, I knew I was a prime candidate. I have heard in the past that it is an awesome and fearful thing to fall into the hands of God. I am a witness that it is an awesome and fearful thing to have him look upon you (even in love) as he did to me that night. I shook violently for a very long time (over fifteen hours?) in his presence. By shaking violently, I mean violent jerking to the point that I could barely smoke a cigarette, and I could not get out more than one word at a time.

As the hours crawled by, God remained eerily silent but undeniably present. After what seemed like days of horrid fear, it surely was only hours, I felt a great peace. The violent shaking continued, but I felt the love of God. I felt that God was telling me that he loved me, and I felt that he was asking me to make a request. I felt assured that any request I made would be granted at that moment. My request came from a trembling heart, "God, I want to serve you, I want to get off meth, and I want to shake the world as your servant."

My request out, I felt like now God had some requests. Call on Jesus was the first and most dominant invitation. My soul shook at the words, but I immediately blew that thought off and smartly replied, "Why would I call on Jesus, a man, when you are God, and you are right here?!" I had heard those words from people over the years, and I was no more receptive to them in the presence of God than I had been on prior occasions.

Regrettably, I would never hear those words again. They may have come, but I refused to listen. God was not into wasting time, so he continued his assault on my pride. Throw away your songs. It was as if God knew that these two requests were not going to be followed. I had worked on my songs for years, there were hundreds of them, and they were my life, my hope, my future as I saw it.

CHAPTER 5
Visions

I'm just going to touch lightly on a few of the visions I had here. The timeline is foggy from this point, but I began to have very vivid visions of things to come. I know this is weird, yet I have complete confirmation through the fulfillment of several of the visions that these were from God. Again, I will only mention them briefly here but may at some point go into deeper detail.

Vision 1: I saw God on his throne in heaven with a white robe that flowed from heaven to the earth. I heard him say, from a great expanse, "Marry Me." I was floored and confused. How could God marry a man? Why would God want to marry a man? What in the world?! I had never heard this before, but the Bible later confirmed from many scriptures that God's followers will be His bride.

Vision 2: I saw a normal-looking door in the clouds, high in the sky, and I was instructed to walk up and open it. When I did, there were millions of people standing behind the normal-sized door in the clouds, and I heard God say, "You will open the door for so many more." That vision quickly faded, and I went directly into a third vision.

Vision 3: I heard the voice again. "I'm sending a beautiful angel to take care of you." I turned my eyes skyward to the right and saw a very beautiful brown-haired angel slowly falling from heaven toward me.

At this point in my life, I was in a goofy awe and had no perception of God's holiness or the drastic seriousness of the current situation. I looked back toward where I had seen God earlier and mocked, "But God, I like blonds!" The fulfillment of this revelation came nearly six years later when I met my wife, who was an exact portrait of that vision. And she is more than I could have ever dreamed of in a woman. Clearly from God.

CHAPTER 6

The Beginning Of Wisdom And Instruction

One thing God said to me during this time was that He had no desire to control my life. This was a big issue for me because I did not want anyone telling me what to do. And by no means did I want to be bound by a book of rules, namely the Bible. God clearly said to me that His only desire was to guide my life and bless me through His wisdom and instruction.

Regrettably, I refused to listen, and a Bible my mother had given me quickly found its way into the trash a few days after that. This was a clear revelation from God in that I have learned over the past twenty-two years of my Christian walk that that is completely true. I had no way of knowing that then. No one had ever said that to me, nor had I read it anywhere. God is good. He's not a control freak looking to set strict rules that no one can follow. He wants us all to be blessed and to live in accord. That's going to take wisdom!

The shaking subsided after what seemed like days. And an undeniable ringing continued to roar through my heart. Throw away your songs, no more drugs, suffer for my name, read the book, marry me. There was a flood of things that came to my mind, and they are not all to be mentioned here. The extraordinary events that would unfold over the next few months would shatter and rearrange my life in a way that I could never have dreamed, and I believe these events will lead to a major life change for the hearts of many in the years to come.

After I had regained my composure, I felt a heavy burden to throw away my songs, and, almost immediately, I felt as if a large clouded presence covered my home. It was god #2, which I now believe to have been the devil or one of his accomplices pretending to be God. This presence crowded in close to me physically and whispered, "Do not listen to him; he is trying to steal your dreams!" Years later, I learned that an evil spirit had been showing up, around this time, at churches in town and pretending to be God. I learned these things much later in my walk with Christ.

Under pressure to act on the instructions God had given, I immediately began to discard everything I owned. Over the next several weeks, I had rid my life of almost every possession that was dear to me. Eventually, the only things I had left in my possession were the only things God asked for—my songs and my heart. I felt pressure from every side of my soul.

About two weeks after discarding all of my belongings, I fell deeper and deeper into despair. I was ready to commit suicide. I walked through the door of my house, ready to end it all. God had a different plan. I was surprised to find that my buddies, who had always been moochers, were there and had planned a huge barbeque party for me with lots of food, drink, and drugs. This threw a bit of a kink in my plans!

When I woke up the next morning, I knew that I had to do something different. I loaded up a few clothes in my junky truck, borrowed a few dollars for gas, and headed east to Arkansas (from Central Oklahoma) with my songs in hand and my heart far from calling on Jesus.

CHAPTER 7

Backwoods Hideout In The Spotlight

I made my way to a backwoods meth production village deep in the mountains of Arkansas to shack up with some of the friends I had acquired over the years. The meth numbed my heart, and I felt good again for a while. I had gotten rid of God. I told myself, "It was just a figment of my imagination." After only a few short days in my new home, the owners of the property had just finished trying unsuccessfully to cook off a fresh batch of meth, poured the waste in the front yard, and left the tools of the trade in the bathtub. Minutes later, dust billowed in the driveway. The cops raided the house. All remained calm. They were looking for a certain individual and did not find what they wanted, but they saw some things they did not expect and surely would be back. I told my buddy, "I think someone just gave us a second chance."

Days of drug abuse rolled on as usual. I had been getting high with my buddy and his girlfriend for a while, and she was laying it on thick with flirting. He was jealous, and it was his house that I was staying in. Bad combination. That night we were forced to come down off of our long meth high, and everyone but me went to bed around four a.m. I was tweaking and paranoid. I was sure that if I went to sleep, my buddy was going to kill me over the girl. People who lived my lifestyle disappeared in this part of the country regularly, and no one seemed to care. Especially the local law enforcement.

I sat in the living room and twisted my last joint of marijuana. As I smoked and slowly enjoyed the transition from speeding to much needed downtime, my eyes fell on a Bible on the coffee table where I read Matthew 6:26-30 which says "Look at the birds of the air; they do not sow or reap or store away in barns, and yet your heavenly Father feeds them. Are you not much more valuable than they? And can any one of you by worrying add a single hour to your life? And why do you worry about clothes? See how the flowers of the field grow. They do not labor or spin. Yet I tell you that not even Solomon in all his splendor was dressed like one of these. If that is how God clothes the grass of the field, which is here today and tomorrow is thrown into the fire, will he not much more clothe you—you of little faith?"

I did not feel God anymore, but I did feel like I was on a crumbling ledge. The logical side of the ledge held pain, devastation, and hopelessness. The irrational side of the ledge held pain, devastation, and a very minute ray of hope. My mind was spinning; why did I open that stupid book?! At this point, I felt the pressure of death to such a point that it was unshakable. I felt that if I did not make a move now (and without alerting anyone), I would soon be in the grave. I cried out to God silently outwardly but screaming within, "I'm going to jump; I will not ask anyone for anything. If you do provide for birds and you are truly there, CATCH ME!" My first thought was that I would go west until I reached the Ocean. Surely that would be long enough for God to prove himself and come to my rescue.

I Cry for Dawn

I live by slinging stones, destroy all who come my way
Supplying evil desires to all willing to play the game
Outside I lead a pleasant life, but my chains were far
from free
The things I use to master men, have now mastered
me

I cry for dawn, send me the sun
I cry for dawn, open my eyes
I cry for dawn, lead me out of the night

I've done all I know to do, and death is drawing near
Deep inside the rot I hide, I'm living in despair
I have to find the courage to get this coward on his
knees
I'm afraid to die with all the hell that lives in me

I cry for dawn, send me the sun
I cry for dawn, open my eyes
I cry for dawn, lead me out of the night

I've nurtured this emptiness, and it's rotting my bones
Love of the night has stolen life's light and all good
known
I hear a battle raging all around me, unseen to human
eyes
I've been pleased with devastation and bound up in
lies

Fearful Father
I've built my life upon decay
My deeds have left deep roots here
And I can't seem to break away

Insight:

I make my living by supplying others with evil and
illegal desires. My life is sustained by destroying the
lives of others. I look wealthy and like I have a great
life, but I am really empty and void. I have fallen
for my own schemes and am in the process of being
destroyed by the work of my own hands. I'm crying out
to someone, somewhere, for some glimmer of hope in
a darkest night. Is there a glimmer of hope? Will the
sun ever shine on my life again? I'm at the end of my

rope. I am working very hard to hide the rot and decay that is quickly destroying everything in my life. I can feel that there is something more happening than what my eyes can see, but I do not know how to fight with the unseen world. I brush these thoughts away and go back to the business of destroying me. I cry out to an unseen creator for help. If He exists, I am begging Him for help.

CHAPTER 8

Holy Ghost Boot Camp

I was deep in the mountains, far away in rural Arkansas. My truck had been impounded days earlier for lack of insurance, so I stepped out onto the curvy and dark mountain highway and pushed my screaming body and mind into the first few steps of what would turn out to be a very long journey. Out of nowhere, a truck came speeding up behind me in the thick blackness and came to a stop in the middle of the road. This was very uncommon. I was rarely able to bum a ride in broad daylight, much less in this desolated area at 4:30 in the morning. Soon I was an hour's drive away from the relative safety of the life I had known. I was in Little Rock, and there was no turning back. I had stepped off the cliff, and I would soon either crash into the rocks below or be embraced by the water of this promise I had grasped for.

Walking down the side of the freeway in downtown Little Rock, I had gained an emotional second wind. I casually walked along a roadside concrete traffic barrier. Happy go lucky, I bounced along, and suddenly I dropped from the three-foot ledge and came crashing down on my knees.

Looking back, I tag this fond memory of severe pain as the introduction to "Holy Ghost Boot Camp" day one. I strolled along, and before I knew it, I was in a big rig and headed for Oklahoma City. I made it to the outskirts of the western side of OKC before midnight and had been on the road for just under twenty hours. I decided to crawl under a bridge ledge and try to get some rest. After an hour or so of tossing and turning, I decided to press on.

After the shelter of the bridge was well out of sight, and as I stared into an endless sea of road, it started to sprinkle, and then it started to pour down rain. As the semi-truck's passed, long sharp whips of rain beat across my back and legs. Welcome to the fury of hell. Turn back now!

I pressed forward with my nose in the grindstone despite an overwhelming urge to give up. If there had been an easy means of escape at that point, I would have likely taken it (this would be true of many points in this journey). My body was screaming for me to just lie down and die, and my mind was demanding that I press on and trust this God into whose hands I had put myself. No sooner had I determined that I would not give up no matter what, a truck stop sign rose from the black night in the distance, it seemed from nowhere. My pace quickened as I could almost feel the warmth of just being out of the freezing March rain and the beatings of the winds from the trucks. A truck stop would be a great place to hang out and wait for a ride.

I walked and walked, and the sign seemed to stay just out of reach. After what seemed like an eternity, I finally reached the exit ramp, and then it took another fifteen minutes or so to finally find what I had thought was a truck stop. I walked up to the dinky gas station, and my hopes of a ride vanished. This was a Loves but not a truck stop, and there was no truck in sight or a place for a truck to get gas let alone to park. I made my way into the bathroom, broke and broken, and soaked up the hot air hand dryer for a few minutes before making my way back outside to the front of the store.

As I stood under the front awning of the store with sheets of rain pouring down heavily, a semi-trailer seemed to appear out of nowhere in the darkness. My heart skipped and then sank as the guy stormed into the store and back out again. For whatever reason as he went back to his truck, he paused and looked back and asked me if I was stranded. I told him I was, and he offered me a ride. After a few minutes of conversation about our days, I learned that the truck driver had been fooled by the large Loves truck stop sign too.

That ride ended, and I spent a painful and cold night in Albuquerque, NM, before moving on to Flagstaff, AZ, late in the evening on day three. I was used to walking ten miles or so with no problem. I'm not sure how much I walked in those few days, but I can tell you that my feet felt like they would explode at any minute. Each step was pure misery.

I walked up to a large truck stop in Flagstaff. The place looked like a five-star hotel to me, with all the fancy furniture, big-screen televisions, and rows of bathrooms for the truckers. I walked past a lovely lady who was very nicely dressed; she was hand in hand with her husband. She must have seen the deep pain in my eyes (both emotional and physical). She stopped to talk with me, and as we departed, she shook my hand and passed me a twenty-dollar bill. That money was my ticket to the first food I had had in quite a while, a hot bath, and freshly washed clothes (I did not take a change of clothes because God was going to clothe me!).

I paid the lady at the cashier desk my seven dollars, stepped into the private shower stall and was shocked to find the biggest bathtub I had ever seen. I filled it with scalding water and soaked my aching body while my clothes washed in the washers in the next room. I slept that night on the couch in front of the big screen TV in the truck stop recreation room. They ran the other homeless folks off, but I was left alone.

I remember only staying there one night, but it seemed like days. I was overwhelmed with dread concerning the thought of being back out on that long lonesome road with my aching feet. I finally forced myself to leave the air-conditioned sanctuary I had found and made my way toward the freeway. As I approached the on-ramp, my mind was overwhelmed with screams, "God is not real; this is stupid, turn back now!" The presence of God that had ultimately led to this horrendous experience was erringly absent, yet by the Grace of God, I let out a loud shout, "God, they are telling me you are not going to help me!" With that, I pressed on and walked down the on-ramp to the freeway.

As I approached the freeway, I saw the steepest and longest hill ever. My heart sank. "No one will stop on this stupid hill," I thought out loud. No more had I set foot on the freeway, then a semi fully loaded with hanging beef stopped. I was in shock and did not think that they could have possibly stopped for me, so I did not rush toward the truck. After a few moments, the truck driver emerged and shouted, "Do you want a ride or not?!" I ran for the truck, and the hooks of God's faithfulness sank a little deeper into my soul.

After a long ride, I had reached my original destination, if I had one that is, Long Beach, CA. I was dropped off in a vast industrial area. Empty despair swarmed all around in my mind and seemed to engulf my body. Here I was. "Hello, I'm in California now, God! I'm at the Ocean. What now?!"

CHAPTER 9
California Dreams

Although I did not realize it at the time, this journey was God's way of separating me from my negative surroundings, all while breaking down a pride-filled heart. In 1991 I did not really believe in God, but I talked to Him, in case he was there, on occasion.

One day I felt very strongly that I needed to go to California. I had no reason for going, so I made a demand upon God to try and verify this feeling of needing to leave my family and friends. One of my favorite songs was "Signs" as sung by Tesla. I had a cassette tape but never recalled hearing that song on the radio. So I said to God, "If you are there and you want me to go to California and leave my family and friends, then let the next song played be 'Signs' by Tesla." I have never heard so many commercials in my life. It seemed like an eternity that I waited for the next song. When the song did come, it was "Signs" by Tesla. I was excited and scared and eventually discredited the idea of leaving my family. I often wonder how my life might have changed if I had escaped all of the negative influences at that time. I might have never taken meth for the first time in the following months? But thanks be to God; He is patient and faithful to pursue us beyond our potential failures.

As I stood on the shore of the Pacific Ocean, I was reminded of having had heard something inside telling me to read the Bible. There seemed to be so many voices fighting for my attention that I had managed to ignore it. But by this point, my flesh was all but dead, and I was but a shred of the pride-filled rebel that had walked out onto the highway four days earlier. I heard clearly inside, "No good thing will happen until you read the book." I was a wanna-be songwriter, so I reasoned that maybe I was supposed to read the dictionary that I had found on the side of the road and come up with a great song that would provide my much-needed salvation. I wanted nothing to do with a Bible. It was confusing and the farthest thing from my mind at the time.

CHAPTER 10

Hello, Anybody Here?

I walked for what seemed like hours and finally made it to a spot on the beach that seemed like a good place to hang out. I had arrived. Now it was God's turn to act. I walked along the beach for a while, and for some reason, I decided to throw away my heavy jacket and my very stinky socks and shoes. That proved to be a painful mistake as darkness approached, the blistering heat of the day faded, and the howling cold winds of the ocean set in, leaving me with nowhere to hide.

I spent that night huddled in an infant-like ball in a construction area under a drafty supply tent. The winds howled, and I cried out to God for mercy. Right on time, as always up to this point, mercy arrived the next day in the form of a local missionary. As I walked along the outside of the tall fence that surrounded the construction area, a man took notice of my plight and loudly asked me if I needed a job. I quickly answered yes but little did I know he, and God, had more in mind than just a job.

This particular fellow had set up a mission in his home for troubled and homeless men. The goal of the program was to stay for one year with the family, during which time all food and shelter would be paid for by working as a group at odd jobs acquired by the missionary. A small portion of the money was given to the individual who was receiving the assistance. This seemed like a great deal. We all sat around, his wife and kids and about ten other homeless men and ate a wonderful and abundant meal that night. I felt that I had finally found the mercy that I was looking for. I was finally in the hands of God.

Unfortunately, my pride and impatience would bleed back through, and I would not be there for long. The family lived upstairs and interacted with the group of men in the lower sections of the house. The men were all to sleep in a large room full of bunk beds, there was a television, but it was not allowed to be used by us, there were many strict rules about conduct and curfews, and a lot of prayers and talk about Jesus. I was not able to get much sleep that first night, and my spirit grew more restless and rebellious as the night grew on. By dawn, I had determined that this was not the place for me and that God surely had another plan. That morning before anyone stirred, I threw my bag of songs over my shoulder, climbed out the window, jumped the retaining wall, and made my way onto the freeway that led to downtown Los Angeles.

CHAPTER 11
When Will I Wait?

I bumped along and made my way back to the beach. As I sat on the park bench pondering my next move and gazing out over the beautiful and vast ocean, I noticed a huge face in the clouds. As I stared at the cloud, it seemed to get closer and closer, and the closer it got, it became clearer that it looked like the face of Jesus, as we often see him represented. In my spirit, I felt strongly that God was telling me to wait patiently on that park bench, possibly for days, for an answer to my prayers. I pondered the previous night spent freezing near the beach in the construction tent and made my way to my feet and promptly left the area.

I often wonder what would have happened if I had waited there for God to answer my prayer. I made my way to a residential part of town, and as I walked along, opportunity leaped upon me again. This time it was in the form of a well-dressed, heavy-set black man covered in thick golden jewelry. He asked me if I needed a place to stay (it was obvious that I did, given my physical state). I approached him to hear out his offer. This particular gentleman had bought a large house with many bedrooms. He used the house to help homeless people acquire welfare benefits and then took the benefits in return for food and shelter. This sounded a lot better than another night in the freezing cold, so I went with the man. I found myself in a large house full of undesirable characters, but there was plenty to eat and a warm bunk bed to sleep in. That night I tried to sleep, but the haunting thought of falsely obtaining welfare benefits (I had only been in the state for a week or so and had to say that I had been there for months) coupled with the fact that I would be breaking my word by physically asking someone for something led me to run from that place the very next day. This is the first time I can remember feeling guilty about breaking the law, much less just thinking about breaking the law. After all, laws were made to be broken, right?

I walked along the streets of L.A. for several hours with no sense of direction or what the future could possibly hold. Evening began to fall, and my heart began to race, wondering if God would come through or if I would spend another night in the freezing cold. As I walked along pondering my fate, an old man pulled alongside me in a fancy car. "You look like you're hungry, am I right?" I quickly nodded and headed toward the car. We visited a local diner where we briefly discussed my plight and my need for a placc to stay for a few days.

As fate would have it, I was in the hands of another opportunist who just so happened to have a very large compound where he lived and also rented out several of the rooms. I felt ecstatic and relieved that I would not be sleeping in the cold, and I had the promise of my own room, which I could work off with maintenance things that needed to be done around the house. Unfortunately, this gentleman had other things in mind for me.

When I arrived at the house, I was shocked to see that there was a very tall metal fence with spikes on top and a large gate with a large padlock. The old man pulled out his huge wad of keys and led me into the inner courts of his front yard. As he locked the huge gate behind me, I felt like I had entered a prison. We walked through the large and creepy front door, and he quickly locked this with a key from the inside. The creep factor grew as I noted that there seemed to be bars and locks on every door, every window, every cabinet, even the television was in a padlocked cabinet.

The creepiness really set in heavy on my spirit as the man's demeanor changed to that of a hungry predator desperate for a meal. His story changed from that I would have my own room to that I would be sleeping in his room and that we needed to go there and get acquainted right away. I maintained my cool, asked for the restroom, and quickly but quietly made my way outside. My heart raced as I wandered through the maze of his gardens and bushes, searching frantically for a route of escape. I pushed my way through a heavy set of hedges and was met with the large fence that stood between me and freedom.

Somehow, I scaled the nine-foot concrete fence and dropped hard onto the other side. I made my way to my feet and started to sprint when I realized I was in another backyard. There was a very large Rottweiler growling at me from a short distance, and there was a man with a shotgun standing on the back porch. Mercy was on my side, and I was able to escape the situation unscathed, except for the fact that my heart was in my throat two or three times over!

That night I made my way back to downtown L.A. prepared to face the bitter cold of the night. I was lucky to find a large dumpster filled with flattened cardboard boxes, and I buried myself inside for warmth. I was good and asleep when I heard the sounds of metal hitting metal, I felt a jolt, and the dumpster began to rise. I was about to be dumped into a recycling truck and crushed! If fate had set one thing straight with me, it was that it was time to leave Los Angeles.

As I walked down the side of the busy freeway in the crisp cold morning air of L.A., I felt an overwhelming sense of loneliness and doom all around me. I walked for hours, from the rising of the sun to the setting of the same. As the hours slowly passed, I continued to be hopeful of some kind of miracle rescue. No rescue ever came. As I left the populated areas and ventured deeper into the vast desert wilderness, it became more and more obvious that I had no water and no hopes of finding any anytime soon. Everything seemed parched and dusty. I had made it out of Los Angeles and deep into a desert that sucked me deeper into its clutches until the cold darkness had surrounded me and night had fallen upon me.

I was in the middle of nowhere, alone, scared, and very cold. I made my way off of the highway, and in desperation to escape the cold, and in defiance of the many colorful signs I had read warning of a strict fire ban, I built a small fire with the scrub brush. It seemed that the fire somehow provided relief even though it was not all that warm. I shivered through the night until the sun peeked over vast mountains, and then I made my way back to the road and continued to head north. As I walked along, I saw a ghostly figure in the distance walking toward me. He was tall and thin with a long beard that was covered in ice. He had spent the night in the same conditions I had, but he had not found the luxury of a small fire. Looking back and knowing the hell that lay in front of me and that from which I had just come, I often wonder where that man came from, where he was going, and if he ever found any relief in this life.

I continued down the highway into the early afternoon with no sign of any sort of ride or help from anyone. I was not asking for a ride. I would have taken one, but one condition I had for proving God was that I would ask no one for anything. I never raised a hand or a thumb one time.

My feet felt as if they would explode at any moment, but my mind was determined to press on. It almost felt like I would die if I stopped moving, and I was still in the middle of nowhere. A glimmer of hope came with sirens and flashing lights that sped in behind me and came to a sudden stop. After a short conversation, the CHP officer offered me a ride, but not the ride I had hoped for. He took me to a desolate exit ramp and dropped me off with a stern warning that I would be taken to jail if I set foot back on the freeway. By this time, I was well over twenty-four hours without anything to eat or drink. And there were no signs of relief in any direction. The voice that was quietly leading me, or perhaps just following me and waiting for my hard heart to be broken enough to listen, made it clear that I was to stay on this desolate exit ramp.

My mind raced at the horrors of just sitting and waiting, and I struggled with thoughts of how to escape my current predicament. The harder I fought to reason my way out of the clear command to stay put, the more I thought about the face of Jesus in the clouds that I had seen three days before, and that clearly told me to stay put in that place and wait for an answer to my prayers. The hell that followed the days after the first time God told me to wait led me to break down, swallow my violent impatience, and wait. I could not help but think of how the hell I had been through for the past few days could have possibly been avoided. Little did I know that this hell would be intensified in the hours to come.

CHAPTER 12
The Heavy Weight Of Waiting

I had been determined to stay put, but I could not sit still, so I paced back and forth down the side of the on-ramp for hours. My mind was racing, and the very little patience I had was being pushed to the brink. Darkness finally fell, and exhaustion consumed me. I decided to go under a pine tree on the side of the ramp and try to lie down and get some sleep. As soon as I stopped moving, the cold consumed me like a flood of ice-cold water. That night I was so cold that I used my hands to dig a shallow hole in the ground. I laid down in the hole, and I covered myself with the dirt in a futile attempt to escape the punishing cold and wind.

After an eternity, my faithful friend, the big beautiful, warming sun, rose and provided a break from my nightly beating. I took my spot back on the on-ramp and began to impatiently pace back and forth. Cars sped up and down the freeway, but there was no traffic whatsoever on this particular entrance ramp for the freeway. I guess not a lot of people are heading deeper into a big empty desert?!

I felt abandoned, and I did not know if God had really spoken to me or if he would ever answer. Would I spend another night here? A week? When would I decide that enough was enough? I had already been nearly 72 hours without food or water. As I paced, a small miracle of mercy welcomed me. The onramp was lined with sprinklers, and they came on, and I drank. At no other time in my life had I been without abundant food and water. This was my first fast, although it was an unintended one.

The sprinklers and the relief they brought disappeared as fast as they came. The damming terror of the freezing night soon gave way to blistering heat. I paced for hours back and forth, up and down the desolate on-ramp. My mind continued to race, and I was wearied from the long cold night with minimal sleep. My feet ached, and my heart seemed to race faster by the minute. My patience was wearing thin, but somehow, I had resolved in my mind that I would stay put. After what seemed like an eternity of pacing in the heat, I gave in to my frustrations and sat down with my back against a road sign on the ramp. Somehow, I fell into a deep sleep.

Blinded Eyes

In a land of deceit
My hands have dealt betray
Hell's bosom's been embraced
And now it's time to pay

Lightning rain your wrath down on me
Shove me from the fire so that I can see
Crush this flesh that I may rise
Free me from these blinded eyes

Father I've not forgotten
I'm asking you remember me
Pluck me from these coals
I'm in way too deep

Lightning rain your wrath down on me
Shove me from the fire so that I can see
Crush this flesh that I may rise
Free me from these blinded eyes

Let the cleansing of your fire
Fall and rip through my soul
Come gather up the pieces
That I may be made whole

Lightning rain your wrath down on me
Shove me from the fire so that I can see
Crush this flesh that I may rise
Free me from these blinded eyes

Insight:

Somewhere beyond my conscious thinking, my mind is praying for me. I am living a life far from actual reality, both the seen and unseen. I am a liar; I lie to steal from others. I do not consider myself a liar or a thief, but I am constantly manipulating others through deceptive practices. My conscience is crying out for a beating that will awaken my flesh to the reality of my life of folly.

CHAPTER 13

On The Road Again

I awoke to the sound of a horn honking in the distance. I looked around with my bloodshot eyes in an effort to locate the source of the confusion and finally saw a junky old van sitting about a hundred feet down the on-ramp from me. Shouts rolled along with the honking, "Hurry up!" I made my way to my feet and rushed to the passenger side of the van. An overwhelming smell of liquor rolled from within and an old fat drunk man slobbered in the passenger side of the van. I looked long and hard, but the driver was seemingly absent. I went for the back door to jump in, and he yelled, "What are you doing?! You're driving!" I made my way to the other side of the van, no driver's license (suspended or revoked, do not remember which), no identification or wallet whatsoever for that matter. I jumped into the driver's seat, and before I could start the motor, he drunkenly mumbled, "Sure am glad you picked me up. I did not think I was going to make it much further."

We drove for an hour or so with the gas tank on empty. When we had gone as far as we dared to with the limited fuel, the drunk began begging for gas money and asked me to do the same. At first, I pretended to entertain the idea in hopes that he would be able to get the money we needed without me having to ask anyone for anything. That was my firm red line!

I went into the store to use the bathroom and get a drink of water. While I was in the store, someone, who could apparently see my severe state of distress, bought me a coke. When I walked out of the store, I found a large bag of Doritos on the ground, and I grabbed them. So here I am, supposed to be begging for money for gas, and I have a coke and a big bag of chips!

When I got back in the van, he showed me the two dollars he had bummed and the suitcases he had stolen from a truck by we were parked. When I was unable to produce any cash, he started yelling about how I had spent the money I had bummed on chips and pop!

We got our two dollars in gas and then went to a grocery store. I had seen enough and was carefully planning my exit strategy. At the grocery store, he again wanted me to beg for gas money, and he became quite aggravated when I said that I would not beg anyone for anything, and he quickly changed the subject to getting some food. We walked into the store together, and he began shoving beer and meat into his pants. I was apparently naive as to what his initial intentions were, but as soon as I saw what he was doing, I left the store.

I intended to grab my bag of songs out of the van and leave before he came out of the store, but the van was locked. When he came back to the van, he drove away without me, and I chased him through the parking lot in an effort to get my bag. I apparently caused enough of a commotion that he was afraid of the attention, and he stopped and threw my bag of songs at me. Or maybe God wanted me to still have an opportunity to obey by throwing them away myself?

That night I felt overwhelmed and distressed about where I was going to sleep. By this time, you would think that I could trust God to come through. He had every time so far. Well, he did again. As I walked out of the small town down the lonesome highway, the sun fell, and a bright moon lit up the night sky. The cold air rushed back in as fast as it had left, and as I walked, I noticed large fields of what appeared to be freshly cut wheat on either side of the road. I ventured out into the field and gathered up several large armloads of the grasses and piled them into a concrete culvert. With a door made of tumbleweed, concrete walls, and a bed of prickly grass, I managed to get a few hours of shallow sleep in the bitter cold.

The next morning when the sun rose, I headed back to the road. To my dismay, I was covered in stickers from the grass from head to toe. I tried in vain to pull the stickers from my shirt, pants, socks, and my long, ratted hair. It seemed that every day brought my pride a little lower. I did not realize it at the time, but I was being externally humbled in order to bring me to a place where I could see my internal state and receive what was being offered to me. I felt overwhelmed, abandoned, utterly defeated, and humiliated as I walked along the road. My clothes were ragged and filthy, I reeked of body odor, my long hair was a hot mess, and I felt hopelessly abandoned.

Every day there seemed to be a flood of visual clues that death and failure were eminent. Today was no different. As I walked along the barren highway, a large sign joined in with the other fearful factors of my plight to deter me from pressing on. The sign was nearly as big a billboard, and it read Caution Entering the Wastelands. Everything inside me screamed for me to press on; my body screamed for me to give up or somehow give in. Honestly, at this point, I do not think there could be any turning back. Where would I go? To whom? Sure, I was lost and destitute, but somehow, I was free. For the first time in my life, I had hope for the future. My life was more treacherous than it had ever been, and yet for the first time in my life, I had hope that things might be different if I did not give up pressing toward my proving of this God who had visited me.

I forced myself to hold my head high and push past the physical and emotional barrier of that sign. As I walked,

I felt an emotional victory and became encompassed by the surpassing beauty that was beyond it. The hills were tall, and the valleys were deep. A sea of beauty but nothingness for as far as the eye could see. And I was on the edge and walking straight into the heart of it.

My reckless abandon was rewarded with mercy in the form of a new red Camaro that came to a sudden stop in front of me on the side of the highway just a few hundred feet past the sign that warned me to turn back. The middle-aged gentleman threw the door open and motioned for me to hurry if I wanted a ride. Once in the car, we started with small talk. He asked how I was doing, and the conversation soon led to my predicament (my obvious state of dire poverty and filth). I explained that I was in this situation by choice. He did not seem to believe me; who would? Why would anyone put themselves in such a situation by choice?

The man asked if I smoked, and I proudly stated that I had quit smoking cigarettes a few weeks back, although it was because I did not have any. He went on to ask if I smoked anything else, and I reluctantly nodded yes. He motioned to the glove box and instructed me to roll a fat joint for myself and to tuck a few away for later. I'm not condoning smoking weed or doing any drugs for that matter (after all, that is half of what got me into this mess in the first place). However, it was a point of mercy in that I was physically destroyed. In such agony, the few tokes of weed managed to provide a little comfort that day. It also gave me the opportunity to do something I had never done before. It allowed me the opportunity to lay the weed down on the altar at a later time.

After a magical ride through the wastelands, the man dropped me off in the middle of a huge broccoli field on the side of the highway. He pointed me toward San Jose, which was about thirty miles from where we were. I never asked anyone for anything up to this point, and I was very hungry. There were people all over the fields picking broccoli, and in the places where they had finished picking, there were still lots of broccoli heads lying on the ground. I had never been a fan of vegetables, but I had also never been without food. The broccoli was irresistible, and I ate my fill.

To my utter disappointment, my belly did not stay full for long. Needless to say, the broccoli had not been washed, and I'm guessing that it was soaked in chemicals. The chemicals tasted bad, and my stomach found them even less appetizing. To keep it pretty, just imagine a filthy homeless punk on the side of the road with his pants around his ankles spraying body contents from both ends. I had been humbled a little more. Each lash from the Father's hand seemed to be followed with a moment of mercy. After I regained my composure and emptied my insides completely, I pressed on down the road.

Tired, scared, and humiliated, I felt like God was telling me that I would thank Him someday for all of this. I did not know why but I felt great peace. I looked up and laughed a painful laugh and said, "God, I do not know why in the world I would possibly thank you for all of this, but I'll just thank you right now!" I had no idea what was going on or why I was going through all of this, or really even if there was a God. I had a pretty good idea that if there was, He would be on the other side of my journey, wherever the other side might have been. That night I was met with the mercy of a pile of trash that was easily constructed into a makeshift tent, complete with a mattress made of nasty old couch cushions. I slept like a baby that night. I was stoned on weed, warm in a tent, on a soft bed, and God was getting closer than ever to having me right where he wanted me.

Beast of Burden

I chose the road I'm traveling
And it's built on jagged stone
I killed a man for no good reason
Now I have to walk alone

I'm a beast of burden
Shackled by my shame
I'm a beast of burden
For the tongue no man can tame
I'm a beast of burden
Please take this yoke from me

The screams I caused that day
Set off a cold silence within
I lie awake at night and wonder
Will I ever taste the light again

I'm a beast of burden
Shackled by my shame
I'm a beast of burden
For the tongue no man can tame
I'm a beast of burden
Please take this yoke from me

I got to break free from these walls
Some say I don't have a chance
The silence is eating away my soul
My heart is held by dead hands

I'm a beast of burden
Shackled by my shame
I'm a beast of burden
For the tongue no man can tame
I'm a beast of burden
Please take this yoke from me

Insight:

My choices have created the life I am living. I killed myself and my dreams through my words, my chosen environment, and my actions. Inside I am very lonely, but I hurt people, and people hurt me, so I have chosen to stay far away from people at all costs.

I'm ashamed of my life. I'm burdened by my ways and by the everbearing fruit of my sin-filled life. I'm begging someone to help me.

CHAPTER 14

The Beginning Of The End

The next morning I set out on the twenty-plus mile hike into San Jose. My feet felt as if they would explode into chunks of hamburger meat at any moment. I pressed on with a limp but trying to maintain my composure. I had walked for a few miles when a tiny car pulled up behind me and honked. It was a little old Vietnamese man with a mouth full of rotten teeth. "Where you go? Like Jack Tripper?" He repeated these two sentences and some other things over and over, but I could not understand what he was trying to say or what he wanted.

Finally, he motioned me toward the car and said, "No more walking for you!" That I understood. And little did he know, he was right. This man gave me a ride into San Jose and gave me a twenty-dollar bill along with his phone number. I promptly went to Burger King and ate real food and then bought a day pass for the bus. I rode the bus through the day and took a leisurely stop at a beautiful nature park with a lake and several waterfalls. I felt as if I was in heaven as I washed my mangled feet under the cool waterfalls. After I had thoroughly aired out my feet, I got back on the bus and rode it until I was forced to get off, very late in the evening. I stood in the roadside bus stop confused and as scared as someone who is leaning fully on a God they do not know can be. Again I found myself hopeless and alone, with no one to ask for help even if I were to consider allowing myself to cross that red line.

The favors of mercy on this trip had a common theme. They always seemed to come when they were least expected, from where they were least expected and least likely, and they always seemed to come suddenly when the need was the direst.

I stood in that bus stop wondering what to do for only a few minutes, when a very large man with a large bottle of what appeared to be liquor in his hand rode past me on a bicycle down the middle of the road. He glanced toward me, and I proudly threw my head back and said, "How's it going?"

He rode on past me a little and then gently turned his bike back in my direction, laid it down on the sidewalk, and got right up in my face with his bottle still in his hand. He was a tall, large, and quite drunk Mexican man, and his hot nasty breath reeked of tequila. He loudly growled, "What did you call me?!"

"I uh just said how's it going…" I replied softly. There was nowhere to turn, as I was cornered between this brick house of a man and the walls of the bus stop. We would have to fight; he would have to eat that bottle of tequila without chewing. One of us was going to die.

After a split second, and after a million thoughts of panic had raced through my mind, He softened his growl. "Where are you staying tonight?" I replied, "I do not know." "I do. It's gonna get cold; you are staying with me." He wrinkled his brow. "Only one night; I cannot afford to have you stay any longer."

That night the drunken Mexican opened up to his own plight. He had been an infantryman in Vietnam, and he had been forced to kill a little girl. The memory of that day brought bitter tears and heart-wrenching pain to him on a daily basis. The story went that he was in the jungle on patrol and his team was about to cross a swinging bridge. As they approached the bridge, a little girl with hand grenades taped to each hand came running across the bridge at the group of men. The Mexican was in front of the team, and his squad leader kept yelling for him to shoot her. He did, and he likely saved several lives, including his own, but his pain was overwhelming and never-ending. He kept asking me if God would forgive him. I did not know much about God, but it sounded reasonable that God would forgive him. I wish I could talk to that man again today. It was clear that he was trying to make up for past mistakes by helping others. Being good does not bring peace to your soul if you do not have Jesus in your heart.

The next day I left, and Mother's Day was fast approaching. I wanted badly to phone home. No one knew where I was, and I later learned that they had given me up for dead due to my history with shady dealings. Many people around me had disappeared in a similar fashion. I knew that if I called home, I would break the commitment that I had made to find God. I would wind up back home in the same mess I was in. It was necessary that I find God before going home, if ever. I compromised by determining that the Vietnamese friend had offered help and given me his number. I did not "ask" for anything, and I would not. I called him and said that I just needed someone to talk to and had intentions of just saying hello and thanks again.

He was ecstatic and would not take no for an answer. He was coming to take me to lunch. Over our meal, he kept talking about Jack Tripper from Three's Company and a travel trailer in his backyard. Truly I could not understand a word he was saying, but I could somewhat make out those two things. From what I did understand, I gathered that he had an extra place for me to stay for a while, and he was eager to have me stay there. When we arrived at his house, things got really weird. He did not have a trailer out back. He had a very nice double-wide trailer in an elite trailer park (never knew there was such a thing). In that trailer, he had an extra bedroom that he offered me to stay in. That all seemed great. And then his wife came home.

I do not think she spoke any English; at least she never did in front of me. The two of them commenced to have a two-hour screaming match, and it was obvious it was because of me. Little did I know that the problem was not just that he was inviting a stranger into the house, but that he was gay and I was the suspected lover? Ooops?!

After the wife left, the little man made his real intentions known, and I made my real intentions known. Thank you for all of your help, and I will be leaving now! To my surprise, when I made it clear that I was not interested in giving what he wanted, he respected my wishes and continued to be adamant about helping me anyway. I was allowed to stay for a few nights, and then the man paid for me to have my own apartment. I was finally to a place where I was broken but could be physically still and listen to God.

CHAPTER 15

Run A Little Farther

The stillness and solitude seemed overwhelming. The same drive that had pushed me out of the door at the start of this journey was as strong as ever. There must be more. I must need to find something else. I determined that that something else could likely be found eight-hundred and fifty miles away in Seattle, Washington.

I stepped out of the comforts of my apartment and walked for about thirty minutes while trying to gather my thoughts and my plan of escape. In desperate frustration, I remembered a remote verse from the Bible, "If you say to this mountain to move and be cast into the sea, it will obey" (paraphrased from memory). I looked up to the rolling white clouds and screamed, "You mountains standing between me and Seattle, be moved and cast into the sea!" I do not know if this was a coincidence or what (there sure was a lot of coincidences on this trip if it was), but I no sooner had the words out of my mouth when I heard an insistent honking. It was the little Vietnamese man.

"Where are you going?!" he shouted out of the car window. "I'm going to Seattle," I replied. "I give you money and buy you plane ticket!" he said. The mountain had been instantly removed.

I quickly made my way to Seattle and found myself more overwhelmed with stress and thoughts of defeat than ever. I had once lived in Seattle and was familiar with the city, but everything seemed foreign and treacherous. I knew deep inside that I had reached the end of my journey. There was nothing left within my power to promote or find the solution to the promotion of my songs which I saw as my only hope for salvation. I had proved God, but it was bitterly empty. I could go on for another year with His Grace leading and blessing me with another thousand miles of turmoil every week. Almost upon arrival in the city, I felt the utter need to turn back. I was at the end of my rope with nowhere left to run. I went straight from the airport to the bus station and took a bus back to my apartment in San Jose. As I lay there on my small cot, I felt the overwhelming conviction of God for the first time. I had enjoyed and blown off the loving presence of God for nearly two months straight with such an overwhelming high that could not be explained just a few months back.

I had felt my conscience off and on throughout my life and was very good at ignoring it. This time it was different. There was no ignoring the feelings. The more I pushed, the more I was consumed by the overwhelming burden of my sin. With one simple sentence, God broke my tattered pride, "You will give an account for every word you have written there in those songs." Simple and to the point.

At first, I thought, no big deal, I will make an adjustment or two, take out a few cuss words, and all will be well. The more I erased, the more I read, the more I became overwhelmed at the absolute evil nature of my songs and my life and mind in general. I fought, I cried, and then I surrendered. It was a simple task that likely would have saved me from the months of hell that I had endured if I had obeyed back in November. I cried out, "God, I will give you what you want…" With that, I proceeded to destroy every last one of my songs and my last joint of marijuana.

I had spent thousands of hours and over ten years writing those songs. My songs were radical and explosive. Death and drugs were the gods I chose to serve and the gods in which I blatantly promoted for others to serve. This was not really a troublesome thought until I met God face to face and realized there was a place in store for people like me. The overwhelming love of God gave me the solution, but I was far from ready to receive it at the time. I needed a little softening up first. And I got it!

CHAPTER 16
Death And A New Day

The songs were gone, and my heart was broken like I had never imagined. I felt a huge void inside. I felt no hope for the future, no reason for living, and yet strangely, I did not feel suicidal as I had in the beginning. My songs were gone, I had thoroughly proved God, and I'd successfully been off of meth for several months. There was no reason to do anything but head home and start over, whatever that meant. I promptly made my way back home as if nothing had happened and went straight to my mother's house.

Within the hour of arriving home, I was greeted by old drug buddies, and I quickly injected meth into my veins. After all of that, I was back to square one. I rolled through the high and felt as if I was on top of the world. Yet something had changed in me, be it ever so slight. I had gained a piece of conscience, and I had determined that I would destroy my own life but that I would not sell any drugs because that would be helping to destroy others' lives. Given the fact that I would not sell any drugs and that I did not have money to buy any drugs, my good buddies promptly ditched me back at my mother's home. I sat in the front yard away from everyone as I slowly came down from the clouds of my intense high. Meth has an enormous euphoric high and an equally enormous crash from those heights. The euphoria was slowly replaced with overwhelming self-conviction and despair. I had failed God, and he surely hated me.

Very early that morning, after everyone was asleep, I made my way to my little sister's room. She always slept with mom, and I did not have a room or a bed in the house. I went to her room and threw myself down upon the neatly made bed. Seemingly from nowhere, I started hearing a song coming from one of her stuffed animals, "Jesus loves me this I know, for the Bible tells me so, little ones to him belong, they are weak, but he is strong." My heart broke, and somehow, I knew that God was not angry with me but that he only wanted me to do the two things he had instructed from the beginning—destroy my songs and call on Jesus. I was not sure how to call on Jesus, but I remembered that there were shows that told you how to do it.

Late the next afternoon, when everyone was away, I flipped through the channels and found The 700 Club. I waited eagerly for the end when Pat Robertson would lead me in the sinner's prayer. I cannot explain how that worked because I really did not feel any different after surrendering my heart to Jesus. I can only tell you that I stopped cursing, and I lost the desire to smoke

(I quickly picked back up the habit when I had the resources), even though I did not realize either of these things were particularly wrong at the time.

The numerous friends that supported me in my life of drugs disappeared. I had tried for years to get away from those people, and I never could. I never told anyone I was quitting dope or that I had become a Christian. God's protective hand was later proved out when I moved into the heart of the small town where I had been a major drug provider at one point and in which I had a lot of family and friend drug addicts. They never darkened my door for the two years I lived in their midst as a new Christian.

Let The Darkness Fade

The sun is spent
The stars have gone away
Blood red coats the sky
The saints are gone, but we're still here
And we ain't had rain for days

I see the footprints of angels
In the ashes of a world in flames
They're warning men to repent of their sin
And turn from their evil ways

Fool-hearted, Forsaken, Forlorn
Sin-filled from the day we were born
We are the wicked
Through and through we are stained
Lover of the lawless
Let the darkness fade

The war has ended
Good men are no more
Cowards wear a mark
Hell's child's in charge
The message is clear
Bow at his feet or die

They want to brand me
I'll die if I don't bow
I ain't afraid of dying
I fear life beyond the ground

There's a man with a Bible
He swears he's found the light
I've never been a God-fearing man
But Lord, I hope he's right
Cause one time I heard the preacher say
One time I saw him kneel and pray
And he said

Fool-hearted, Forsaken, Forlorn
Sin-filled from the day we were born
We are the wicked
Through and through we are stained
Lover of the lawless
Let the darkness fade

Insight:

The world is devastated from a great war. Fires have consumed everything. The sky is black at midday due to thick smoke clouds and is only lit by the fires upon the earth. Angels are roaming the earth looking for the remnant of men who will repent and be saved. I feel like a fool that has been abandoned on this earth and left to die alone and without the love of a living God. The wars have stopped, and the One World order is in effect. Only those who worship the new earthly master may eat or drink. My glimmer of hope seeing a man of God leading others in a simple prayer of repentance. I feel fool-hearted, forsaken, and forlorn. I know I have been sin-filled before I even opened my eyes after birth. I know I am wicked. I know I am stained. I know the true God loves everyone, and I am asking Him to let the darkness fade (i.e., open my eyes to the truth of the Gospel of Jesus Christ).

CONCLUSION

This is by no means every detail of these nine months of bliss and hell in my life. I have tried for over twenty years to put this on paper and make it shareable for the benefit of others. I have determined that waiting on every detail of the story to be perfectly explained is not the answer. I'm going to put it out there, and with time and God's favor, we may publish a second version full of more wonderfully interesting stories about God's faithfulness.

The bottom line of this story is that God is real, and God is faithful to his word. If you still have a hard time believing that God exists, I challenge you to call out to him and ask him to reveal himself to you. Read the Bible, visit a local church, or better yet, just call on Jesus right now.

I, too, was a skeptic even in the face of God himself telling me to call on Jesus. God instructed me to lay down the things of this world that held my affection and to turn my eyes to Jesus. Just as was told to me, no good thing happened to me until I called upon Jesus and read his word—the Holy Bible.

Maybe you are living your own life of living hell right now. Maybe God is telling you to call on Jesus. I am 100% confident that if I had called on Jesus when God first revealed Himself to me and pointed me toward His Son, I could have avoided several months of misery that followed my blatant defiance of that command. God is there, but there is only one way to interact with Him, and that is through Jesus. I have been clean for over twenty-two years, and my life is a living testament to God's goodness and faithfulness.

Join me in this joyful journey.

God Loves You!

"This is how much God loved the world: He gave His Son, His one and only Son. And this is why: so that no one need be destroyed; by believing in Him, anyone can have a whole and lasting life." John 3:16

"The thief comes only to steal and kill and destroy; I have come that they may have life, and have it to the full." John 10:10

Sin Separates Us From God

"…for all have sinned and fall short of the glory of God." Romans 3:23

Jesus Is The Only Way To God

"Jesus answered, "I am the way and the truth and the life. No one comes to the Father except through me."
John 14:6

Call on Jesus!

"Yet to all who did receive Him, to those who believed in His name, He gave the right to become children of God." John 1:12

"If you declare with your mouth, "Jesus is Lord," and believe in your heart that God raised Him from the dead, you will be saved." Romans 10:9

ABOUT THE AUTHOR

J.W. LINDER is a husband, father and servant of the Lord. His vision is to see individuals equipped in their body, soul and spirit in order to accomplish their purpose. J.W. is a two-time combat veteran as an infantryman; as well as an entrepreneur, speaker, and songwriter. He has three degrees, including a Master's Degree in Nursing Leadership and Management. For more info and to connect with J.W. Linder visit cryofdawn.com.